CORNERSTONES OF FREEDOM™

THE EUROPEAN INDUSTRIAL REVOLUTION

BY MICHAEL BURGAN

CHILDREN'S PRESS®
An Imprint of Scholastic Inc.
New York   Toronto   London   Auckland   Sydney
Mexico City   New Delhi   Hong Kong
Danbury, Connecticut

BRINGING HISTORY to LIFE

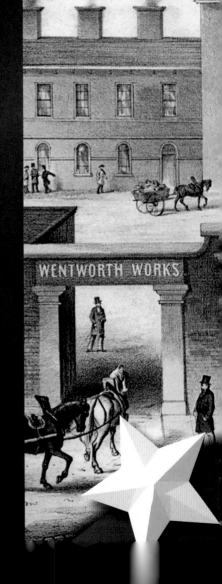

WENTWORTH WORKS

Content Consultant
James Marten, PhD
Professor and Chair, History Department
Marquette University
Milwaukee, Wisconsin

Library of Congress Cataloging-in-Publication Data
Burgan, Michael.
 The European industrial revolution / by Michael Burgan.
 pages cm.—(Cornerstones of freedom)
 Includes bibliographical references and index.
 Audience: 9–12
 Audience: Grades 4 to 6
 ISBN 978-0-531-28202-1 (lib. bdg.) — ISBN 978-0-531-27667-9 (pbk.)
1. Industrial revolution—Europe—Juvenile literature. 2. Industrialization—
Europe—Juvenile literature. 3. Europe—Economic conditions—Juvenile
literature. I. Title.
 HC240.B873 2013
 330.94'025—dc23   2013002134

All rights reserved. Published in 2014 by Children's Press, an imprint of
Scholastic Inc.
Printed in the United States of America 113

SCHOLASTIC, CHILDREN'S PRESS, CORNERSTONES OF FREEDOM™,
and associated logos are trademarks and/or registered trademarks of
Scholastic Inc.

1 2 3 4 5 6 7 8 9 10 R 23 22 21 20 19 18 17 16 15 14

Photographs © 2014: AP Images: 14 (North Wind Picture Archives), 48;
Boeing Images: 55; Bridgeman Art Library: 40 (Archives Charmet), 5 bottom,
10 (Cheltenham Art Gallery & Museums, Gloucestershire, UK), 36 (Look and
Learn), 15 top, 13, 18; Getty Images: 47 (Fotosearch), 11 (Frank Meadow
Sutcliffe/Hulton Archive), 54 (MPI), 16 (SSPL), 27 (The British Library/
Robana), back cover (Topical Press Agency); Oxfordshire County Council
Photographic Archive: 33; Science Source: 21, 56; Shutterstock, Inc./Nicku:
32; Superstock, Inc.: 45 (Album/quintlox), 8 , 46 (DeAgostini), 2, 3, 34, 58
(Everett Collection), 38 (Image Asset Management Ltd.), cover, 6, 15, 24, 28,
30, 31, 43, 49, 50, 51, 57 top, 57 bottom (Science and Society), 7, 44 (The Art
Archive), 42 (Universal Images Group); The Granger Collection: 4 bottom, 12,
20, 26, 35, 37, 41; The Image Works: 4 top, 29 (The Print Collector/Heritage),
52 (World History/Topham); XNR Productions, Inc.: 52, 53.

Did you know that studying history can be fun?

BRING HISTORY TO LIFE by becoming a history investigator. Examine the evidence (primary and secondary source materials); cross-examine the people and witnesses. Take a look at what was happening at the time—but be careful! What happened years ago might suddenly become incredibly interesting and change the way you think!

Contents

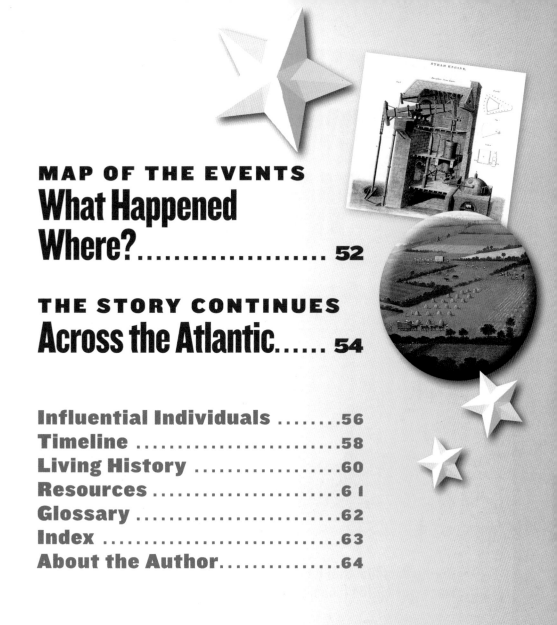

New Ways of Working

During the Industrial Revolution, factories were set up where huge machines called looms wove cotton and wool yarn into cloth.

Across a factory floor in England, men, women, and children stood at machines that whirred almost nonstop. Powered by rushing river waters outside, the machines turned raw cotton and wool into yarn. The yarn was then made into **textiles**.

These workers and machines were part of the **Industrial** Revolution. Starting in the middle of the 18th century, changes in farming, technology, and transportation helped create a shift in the world's **economy**. Before this revolution, most people worked on farms. They often made their own tools and clothing.

The Industrial Revolution replaced human **labor** with machines. It also provided the means to power those machines by fuel, rather than by humans or animals. Farms were able to produce more food with fewer workers. This led to an increase in the number of people available to work in factories or other businesses. In addition, new transportation systems made it easier to move people and goods quickly over long distances.

Before the Industrial Revolution, European farmers relied on animals to power their plows.

THE TERM "INDUSTRIAL REVOLUTION."

CHAPTER 1

FROM THE FARM TO THE FACTORY

Feudalism was once common in many European countries.

FOR CENTURIES, MOST PEOPLE in England lived as farmers. These farmers owed some of the crops they produced to wealthy landowners who ruled over small areas. The landowners, in turn, let the farmers use their mills to grind grain and offered them military protection from enemies. But the farmers who worked for the landowners had limits on their freedom. This system, called feudalism, began to end in England after the 1300s, giving more people control over the crops they raised. If farmers had more crops than they needed for their families, they could sell them at markets.

New and improved farming methods spread throughout the English countryside in the decades leading up to the Industrial Revolution.

Changes on the Farm

During the 17th and 18th centuries, England experienced what has sometimes been called an **agricultural** revolution. This period saw a huge change in farming methods, leading to an increase in crop production. As farmers in one area improved their production, farmers in other parts of the country borrowed their methods. This process of spreading new and better ways of farming continued into the 19th century.

The agricultural revolution was one of the developments that sparked the Industrial Revolution. The agricultural changes affected many people. In 1700, 80 percent of the English made their living in agriculture. That number dropped to 22 percent by 1850, yet England could still produce enough food to feed its growing population. Because food there was not as expensive as in other parts of Europe, more people had money to buy goods, such as textiles, made by other people. The increased demand for manufactured goods and the rise in population played a part in shaping the Industrial Revolution in England.

The New Methods

The English learned some of their new farming methods from the Dutch. These methods included better ways to drain swampy land so it could be used to raise crops. Farmers also added to their land by cutting down woods and turning pastures into fields.

The crops the farmers raised were important, too. The English began to plant more clover, which adds nitrogen to the soil. Nitrogen is a chemical that helps crops grow. When farmers

By the 19th century, fewer farmworkers were needed to produce enough food for the people of England.

raise crops such as grains, nitrogen is taken out of the soil. Growing clover during one season made the soil better for growing other crops the next season. The clover could also be used to feed livestock, such as cattle.

Farmers learned how to rotate where they grew their different crops to keep the soil healthy. In the past, some of a farmer's land went unplanted each season, to try to rebuild the soil. Crop rotation kept more land in use. This helped increase crop production.

Another change in English farming was the enclosing of farms. New laws required farms to be fenced in. Many

Livestock need plenty of open space for grazing.

farmers without much money could not afford to build fences, so they sold their land to wealthier people who already owned large farms. Larger farms could produce more food at a lower cost than the small farms could. The new laws also ended the practice of keeping areas of land, called commons, for anyone to use. Farmers could no longer let their livestock graze on the commons. The changes meant that fewer landowners could make a living in farming. Former farmworkers became the source of labor for the factories that began to appear during the second half of the 18th century.

TODAY'S PERSPECTIVE

For years, history books talked about the role several English thinkers and inventors played in their country's agricultural revolution. Some history books once taught that Charles "Turnip" Townshend helped introduce turnips to England from Germany. But we now know that turnips were already growing in England when Townshend was a boy. However, Townshend did help show that turnips, like clover, were useful in strengthening the soil.

Other history books praised Jethro Tull (above) for inventing the first seed drill, a machine that made it easier to plant seeds. But simpler seed drills had been used before Tull made his, and Tull's drill was not widely used until the 19th century.

Early Manufacturing

Not everyone was a farmer before the agricultural revolution came to England. There and throughout Europe, skilled craftspeople made goods such as metal eating utensils or wooden furniture. English farmers also produced some goods for sale, such as wool from their sheep. In a part of England called Yorkshire, the most successful wool producers hired people to spin the wool into yarn. The hired workers did the spinning in their own homes using the same simple tools that had been used for centuries.

In 1733, John Kay invented a new type

YESTERDAY'S HEADLINES

Daniel Defoe (above) wrote *Robinson Crusoe* and other novels. He also wrote about life in England. Here's part of an article that he wrote in 1729 on English success in farming:

"The extraordinary increase which our lands, under an excellent cultivation, generally yield . . . is an uncommon argument for the industry of the husbandmen [farmer]; . . . the diligence and success of our husbandry in England will be found to be beyond that of the most industrious people in Europe."

of loom that improved the spinning process. Looms are machines used to weave yarn into cloth. They had been used for centuries. With Kay's "flying shuttle" loom, weavers used their feet in addition to their hands to help control the machine. Work that once required two adults could now be done by one, with help from a child. The Industrial Revolution would soon expand on the idea of using new and better machines to produce more goods with fewer workers or to produce goods faster.

Flying shuttle looms allowed users to weave wider cloth than earlier looms did.

15

CHAPTER 2

NEW POWER SOURCE, NEW FACTORIES

Coal miners faced constant danger from explosions, tunnel collapses, and other risks.

DEEP UNDERGROUND, MINERS stood in water up to their waists as they chipped away at the black coal that surrounded them. The deeper the miners went into the earth to get the coal, the more water seeped into the mines. Simple pumps powered by horses removed some water, but not enough to keep the mines dry.

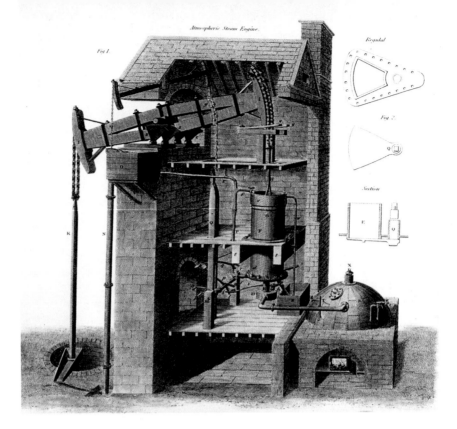

The first known example of Thomas Newcomen's steam engine was built in Staffordshire, England, in 1712.

The English had been mining coal for centuries, but the demand for it increased during the 17th century. Coal, like oil (petroleum) and natural gas, is a **fossil fuel**. It is formed by decaying plants that lived hundreds of millions of years ago. The English burned it to heat metals and shape them into tools. Coal became increasingly important as the English began running out of the wood they had been using as fuel.

Making Iron

At the beginning of the 18th century, Thomas Newcomen invented the first practical steam engine. Using coal for fuel, this engine boiled water to create steam. The steam helped power pumps that removed water from coal mines. Newcomen's engine was more powerful than earlier types of engines. That meant miners could dig deeper than ever before.

Newcomen's steam engine had other uses besides pumping water out of mines. It could be used to power bellows, which produced the air that fed the fires at ironworks. Iron smiths needed high heat to turn iron ore into **molten** metal. The molten iron could then be poured into molds to make such things as pots and tools. In the past, most ironworks were near rivers so they could use the flowing water to turn wooden wheels. The wheels then powered the bellows. Using a steam engine for power meant ironworks could be located anywhere. It made sense to place them near coalfields because coal powered the engines and fed the fires. The use of Newcomen steam engines grew during the 18th century, with hundreds of them soon working in England. Some appeared in Belgium, France, and other parts of Europe, too.

A FIRSTHAND LOOK AT
COALBROOKDALE BY NIGHT

The birth of industrialization changed how England looked. One famous painting of the Industrial Revolution is *Coalbrookdale by Night* by Philip James de Loutherbourg. Coalbrookdale was the site of Abraham Darby's ironworks, and the town remained a center of iron making, with furnaces burning through the night. See page 60 for a link to view the painting online.

Abraham Darby's (right) coke-fired smelting process made it possible to manufacture iron into thinner shapes.

In 1709, Abraham Darby helped ironworks in another way. He found a better way to produce coke, a substance created when coal is burned. He then used coke as fuel during the **smelting** process, which turns the iron molten. This process allowed ironworks to produce iron more quickly and at a lower cost. Creating iron in this way spread slowly, as not all kinds of coal were good for making coke. Plus, smelting with coke required high temperatures that some mills could not produce. Only with time did **engineers** create the technology to solve that problem.

Watt's Engine

As helpful as Newcomen's steam engine was to early industrialization, James Watt thought he could make a better one. In 1769, he received a **patent** for his design. Watt's steam engines could produce more power with less fuel than Newcomen's did. Later Watt engines could also spin a shaft, while Newcomen's could only move a pump up and down. A rotating engine had many uses in industry, such as powering machines that spin thread and weave cloth.

SPOTLIGHT ON

James Watt

Born in Scotland, James Watt began his career making compasses and other small tools used by mathematicians and sea captains of the day. In his business, he met many scientists and became familiar with the Newcomen steam engine. When Watt saw that Newcomen's engine wasted power, he decided to build a better one. Several years after designing his engine, he received money from an industrialist, someone who made money building and running factories. With that money, Watt built his first engines and became wealthy himself. He continued to make improvements to his engine until 1790.

The use of the Watt engine spread slowly in England. Newcomen's engine was still used in many places. But Watt's engine became popular in the growing textile industry, especially for processing cotton. In the years since Newcomen had created his engine, technology

James Hargreaves's spinning jenny machines could spin multiple threads at once.

in textiles had changed quite a bit. Combining new spinning machines with steam power in factories marked the true start of the Industrial Revolution.

New Machines for Textiles

As the demand for cotton grew during the 18th century, manufacturers sought faster ways to spin thread. During the 1760s, the English inventors James Hargreaves and Richard Arkwright built new spinning machines. Hargreaves's machine was called a spinning jenny. It was powered by hand. Turning a crank let a person turn the spindles that spun cotton into thread. Arkwright's machine was called a water frame. Powered by waterwheels, the water frame had almost 100 spindles. Arkwright built mills to house the water frames and hired people to run them. These were some of the first factories. By the 1780s, Arkwright was using steam engines to power his spinning machines.

With new factories turning out more cotton, prices for cotton goods fell. More people could afford to buy this comfortable, easily washable cloth. British cotton goods were traded around the world. The raw cotton came from overseas, including the United States. The early part of the Industrial Revolution had international roots, even if industrialization had not spread far beyond England.

A VIEW FROM ABROAD

U.S. treasury secretary Alexander Hamilton played a key role in promoting industry in the newly formed United States. In 1791, he offered this view of the industrialization taking place in Great Britain:

"The employment of machinery forms an item of great importance in the general mass of national industry . . . . The cotton mill, invented in England within the last twenty years, is a signal illustration of [this] . . . . [A]ll the different processes for spinning cotton are performed by means of machines, which are put in motion by water . . . .To this invention is to be attributed essentially the immense progress which has been so suddenly made in Great Britain in the various fabrics of cotton."

CHAPTER 3

ON THE MOVE

The Canterbury and Whitstable Railway began operation in 1830.

WITH FEWER FARMERS GROWING more crops and steam-powered machines beginning to speed up manufacturing, the Industrial Revolution was taking off in England. But another key change was needed to help push the revolution along. Once again, English industrialists helped lead the way, spending money to build new **canals**. Around the same time, inventors saw the value of using steam engines to power vehicles. This led to one of the greatest inventions of the era: the railroad.

English traders purchased large amounts of tobacco grown on plantations in the American colonies. Here, barrels of tobacco are being loaded on ships for transportation to England.

Waterways for Trade

During the 17th and 18th centuries, England's government knew how important trade was for the country. British ships traveled the world to get natural resources, such as cotton. Some resources, such as timber, came from the American colonies. Members of Parliament, the country's lawmakers, often passed laws meant to boost trade. As the Industrial Revolution began, Parliament passed laws that helped industrialists and farmers move resources and goods within England.

The changes in iron making and the use of steam power meant more coal had to be transported from mines to smelters and factories. For textiles, more raw cotton had to get from port cities such as Liverpool and Bristol to the mills. Then the finished goods had to be brought to ports so they could be sold overseas. Farmers also needed to get their crops to customers across the country. One solution for these transportation issues was to build more roads. Even more important were new canals, since boats could hold large amounts of goods.

Canals have existed for centuries. They can connect rivers, go around parts of a river that are hard for ships to navigate, or link a city to a river or port. In 1759, Parliament passed a law authorizing the construction of a

Liverpool's first dock was constructed in 1715, and the city grew to become one of England's busiest ports by the end of the century.

canal that would directly help industrialization. The canal was named for the Duke of Bridgewater, who owned coal mines near the city of Manchester. The Bridgewater Canal was almost 40 miles (64 kilometers) long. The new canal made it easier for more coal to reach Manchester, and the price of the fuel began to drop.

For most of the 18th century and into the 19th, new canals were dug to link mines and ports with growing industrial cities. At times, wealthy men helped pay for the canals when it would serve their business interests. This kind of **investing** was part of the Industrial Revolution, too. More so than people in other countries, the English had the freedom and the desire to invest money as they chose. They risked their own money hoping to make more.

The Bridgewater Canal originally stretched between the towns of Worsley and Manchester, and in 1776 it was expanded to reach Liverpool.

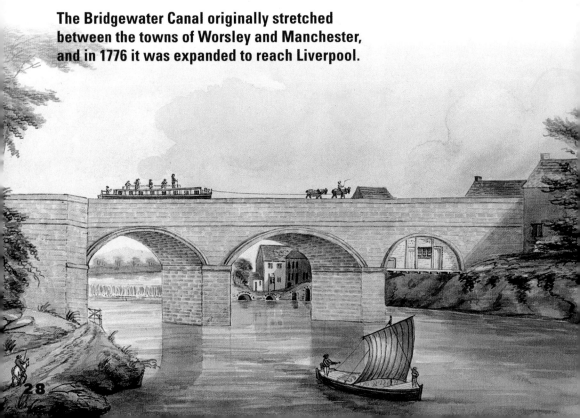

London was home to many factories that produced textiles and a wide variety of other goods.

By the 1780s, new roads and canals linked many of England's northern cities to ones in the middle of the country. Those central cities were connected to the capital, London. Better transportation made it easier for manufacturers to sell their goods within the nation or overseas. As the demand for goods, especially textiles, rose, more wealthy people were willing to invest in the new machines and steam power. More machines meant more goods being produced, which led to lower prices and even more demand.

Richard Trevithick tested his first steam-powered vehicle by driving it up a hill on December 24, 1801.

The Railroad

Coal mines in England sometimes used carts that ran on tracks to haul coal. Horses pulled these carts along the tracks. With the improvements to Watt's steam engine, inventors began trying to use steam power to once again replace the horse.

Richard Trevithick found a way to increase the power from a steam engine. He put the steam under higher pressure than Watt had, which meant a smaller engine could produce more power than Watt's engine. The higher pressure also made a steam engine more likely to explode, but Trevithick thought that having a smaller, more powerful engine was worth the risk.

A FIRSTHAND LOOK AT
STEPHENSON'S *ROCKET*

George and Robert Stephenson's *Rocket* locomotive reached speeds that were uncommon for its time. The original locomotive is on display in London's Science Museum. See page 60 for a link to view it online.

In 1801, he built a small vehicle powered by steam. It was the first locomotive. Two years later, Trevithick opened the first railway to use a steam locomotive. It was located at an ironworks and could carry more than 10 tons of material for 10 miles (16 km). This was much more than a horse-powered cart could carry.

George Stephenson began designing and building improved steam locomotives in 1814. By 1825, he had

In 1808, Trevithick demonstrated his most recent engine design on a circular track in London.

built a railway meant to carry passengers, not just coal and iron at mines and factories. The railroad linked the towns of Stockton and Darlington. Four years later, he and his son, Robert, built a locomotive nicknamed *Rocket*. It could reach speeds of around 30 miles (48 km) per hour. Stephenson had shown that carrying goods and people on trains was faster than other forms of transportation. The idea of public railways soon spread to the United States. The first public railway in the United States opened in 1830.

Before his success in the railroad industry, George Stephenson earned money by repairing clocks and shoes.

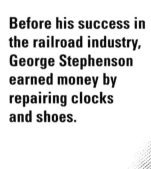

Protesting the Industrial Revolution

Not everyone in England approved of the changes that came with industrialization. Skilled weavers and other textile workers feared losing their jobs. They saw that people with little skill could be trained to run machines, and industrialists didn't have to pay them much for the work. The machines also produced more goods than a person could. A factory with 200 looms powered by steam could do the work of 875 people weaving by hand, and the factory needed far fewer workers to run the looms.

YESTERDAY'S HEADLINES

Angry about job losses, in 1786, textile workers in Leeds published a letter protesting the use of machines for scribbling, a part of the process of preparing wool for spinning. Here is some of their letter:

"The number of Scribbling-Machines . . . exceed all belief, being no less than *one hundred and seventy*! and as each machine will do as much work in twelve hours, as ten men can in that time do by hand . . . and they working night-and day, one machine will do as much work in one day as would . . . employ twenty men . . . we allow four men to be employed at each machine twelve hours, working night and day, will take eight men in twenty-four hours; so that . . . twelve men are thrown out of employ for every single machine used in scribbling."

Smoke from iron and steel factories turned the skies black in English cities such as Sheffield.

For the people who did get jobs in the factories, the workday could last more than 12 hours, with little or no time for breaks. Inside some mills, the temperature could reach more than 80 degrees Fahrenheit (26.7 degrees Celsius). Outside a factory or ironworks, the air was often black from burning coal. As people moved to larger towns and cities to take jobs, they lived crowded together in cheap buildings where disease was common. Leaving the countryside for the cities, people no longer had their own land to grow a few crops. If they lost their jobs or prices rose, it was harder for them to feed themselves.

Protests against the new factories and work conditions sometimes led to violence. Angry workers burned down a Manchester factory in 1795. In the early 1800s, people known as Luddites destroyed some machines. Today, people opposed to new technology are sometimes called Luddites.

Child Labor

Going into the 19th century, some people in Great Britain also began to protest child labor. Since the beginning of industrialization, large numbers of women and children worked in factories. Mill owners could pay these workers less than they did adult men, and they were easier to manage. By 1816, half the workers in British cotton mills were under age 16, and some were under 13. They

Child labor remained common in Europe and the United States until the 20th century.

TODAY'S PERSPECTIVE

The Luddites were named for Ned Ludd, who was said to have led rebellions in factories across parts of England. Historians are unsure whether Ludd was a real person, but his tale spread among 19th-century textile workers. Decades before, Ludd had supposedly become angry with his boss and destroyed his machine. That story fueled the protesters who emerged around 1811.

The idea that the Luddites hated the new technology of the Industrial Revolution is not true. The Luddites only attacked machines owned by industrialists who did not meet their demands. The workers wanted new people on the job to receive training. They also wanted fair wages for their work. The protests came as many workers could not afford to buy food.

faced the same long hours as adults and sometimes were injured running the machines.

An 1802 law tried to protect orphans from the worst conditions of the factories. Before this, many orphans were forced to work at no pay. A later law said that no children under age nine could work in a cotton mill, and another law limited the number of hours women and children could work in a day. In some cases, industrialists began hiring fewer children for another reason—they no longer needed them. Bigger and better machines required fewer workers to run

Union workers sometimes went on strike, or refused to work, until their demands were met by employers.

them. And **unions** also played a part. The unions were led by adult men, and they pressured industrialists to hire men rather than women and children.

The Industrial Revolution brought great wealth to some inventors and mill owners. It also changed the nature of work and the way many people lived. While some workers suffered, others entered what was called the middle class—a group of workers whose wealth was in between the very poor and the very rich. Through the 19th century, more people in England entered the middle class. At the same time, the Industrial Revolution was spreading across other parts of Europe.

CHAPTER 4

A REVOLUTION SPREADS

Nicolas-Joseph Cugnot's three-wheeled car is considered to be the first automobile ever created.

IN 1771, PEOPLE LINED THE streets of Paris, France. They were watching an early test of a steam-powered passenger vehicle. The French engineer Nicolas-Joseph Cugnot hoped his three-wheeled car would replace horses for pulling army cannons. During this test, however, the vehicle somehow lost control and crashed into a wall. That accident, along with the end of the project's financing, ended Cugnot's dream.

In the late 18th century, French foundries manufactured cannons for the French military to use in wars with neighboring countries.

Not all the inventions of the Industrial Revolution were made in Great Britain. Into the 19th century, engineers and inventors in several European countries helped create new methods and machines that increased the pace of industrialization.

Learning from the British

Europeans saw the money Great Britain was making because of industrialization. That money helped finance stronger militaries at a time when European nations competed for influence and new colonies. The English had earlier borrowed farming ideas from the Dutch. Now European nations began to copy British industrial methods where they could. But the spread of industrialization across Europe was slow. France, Belgium, the Netherlands, and Germany were the first to take advantage of the new methods.

Even in the early years of industrialization, some European leaders could see the economic changes taking place in Great Britain. In 1764, France sent one of its scientists to England to study new methods of making iron. With that new knowledge, France started a large, modern ironworks of its own. Some of the new textile machinery also reached Belgium and Germany. In general, though, the British worked to prevent other nations from learning their

Founded in 1811, Germany's Krupp steel company was one of the world's leading steel suppliers until World War II.

new methods. Parliament passed laws that made it illegal for people working in textile mills to go to other countries and share their knowledge about the machines.

European nations tried to get around the British laws. At times, they sent spies to study how machines were made or to sneak machines out of the country. Other times, they offered money to British citizens to ignore their country's laws and help them. Some countries simply bought British goods. For example, George Stephenson sold his rail locomotives to many countries. Despite the laws, a British industrialist named William Cockerill brought textile

British textile workers were forbidden from spreading knowledge of how their machines worked to foreign nations.

British locomotives were loaded onto ships and sold to other European nations. This engine is being shipped from Newhaven, England, to France.

machines to France and Belgium. He then built a factory to make the machines. With British influence, textile mills spread across parts of France and Belgium, where weaving had long been done by hand.

A FIRSTHAND LOOK AT
THE *MECHANICS' MAGAZINE*

For several decades during the 19th century, readers who wanted to know more about the great inventions of the day turned to the *Mechanics' Magazine*. See page 60 for a link to view an issue of the magazine online.

During the Industrial Revolution, the French military leader Napoleon Bonaparte waged war against Great Britain, Austria, and many other European nations, until he was defeated in 1815.

For several decades, starting with the French Revolution of 1789, many European nations were at war. The major forces during these wars were France and Great Britain, who had been rivals for many years. The fighting slowed the transfer of knowledge from Great Britain to the rest of Europe. But during the wars, governments in France and parts of Germany changed their laws to allow workers to go where they wanted to work. The new laws also made it easier for businesses to use new technology. These freedoms helped boost industrialization when the wars ended in 1815.

France and Germany

Geography had played a key role in Great Britain's industrialization. The country had large amounts of coal to use as a source of power. The areas in the rest of Europe where the Industrial Revolution began also tended to have vast amounts of coal. This was especially true in Germany's Ruhr Valley. The amount of coal mined there and in other regions almost doubled during the 1830s. But industrialization was delayed because Germany at the time was divided into hundreds of small independent states. New laws that made it easier to trade goods among the states slowly helped boost the turn to industry.

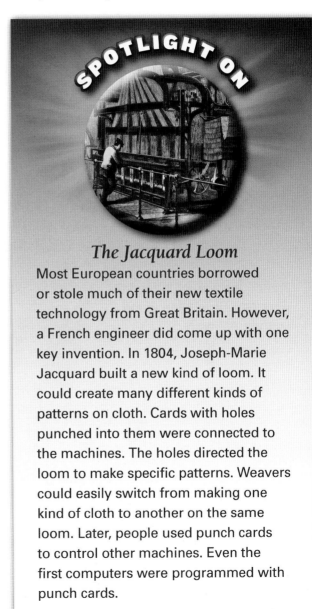

SPOTLIGHT ON

The Jacquard Loom

Most European countries borrowed or stole much of their new textile technology from Great Britain. However, a French engineer did come up with one key invention. In 1804, Joseph-Marie Jacquard built a new kind of loom. It could create many different kinds of patterns on cloth. Cards with holes punched into them were connected to the machines. The holes directed the loom to make specific patterns. Weavers could easily switch from making one kind of cloth to another on the same loom. Later, people used punch cards to control other machines. Even the first computers were programmed with punch cards.

The coal in Germany fired new ironworks, and railroads quickly spread. The governments built most railways and gave banks money to loan to investors. Wealthy citizens also invested in the new industries. The German states had several important rivers for moving goods, and they built canals as well. The growth truly boomed after 1870, when the various German states united into one country.

France, the largest country in western Europe, was also slow to industrialize. The continental wars delayed development, and the country did not have the huge supplies of coal that Great Britain had. To make matters worse, in 1871 France lost a war to Germany and had to give away lands that contained coal.

France lost valuable land to Germany during one of the continental wars.

Le Bon Marche (French for "the Good Market") was one of the world's first department stores, offering a large variety of goods to shoppers.

Still, France did adopt machines for making textiles and increased its iron production. In 1842, the French decided to build a national railway, which increased the demand for iron. France also created one of the first department stores, which opened in the 1830s in Paris. Shoppers wanted to save time by being able to buy many goods in one store. Before department stores, they had to go to separate stores for different kinds of items.

In 1862, the German Krupp company built the first Bessemer-style steel plant outside of England.

The New Industrial Metal

In England, an inventor named Henry Bessemer designed a new shell for cannons that was more accurate than cannon balls. But the shells had to be fired from guns much larger than existing ones. The new cannons would require a lot of steel.

Steel is made from iron, but it is both stronger and lighter than iron. However, making steel was slow and expensive. In 1856, Bessemer discovered that blowing cool air into hot molten iron produced large amounts of steel very quickly. What once took a whole day could now happen in minutes. More steel could be produced in less time. This made the metal less expensive. Cheap steel was now available for railways, machines, and items that no one had even imagined yet, such as the frames of skyscrapers.

A German living in Great Britain, William Siemens, made the next big breakthrough. He invented a new furnace that burned at higher temperatures while using a cheaper kind of coal. This made metal production even cheaper. Siemens's invention was first used to make steel in 1864 by Pierre-Émile Martin of France. The Siemens-Martin method of making steel was even more popular that Bessemer's. It produced higher quality steel, though it was slower than Bessemer's method.

SPOTLIGHT ON

The Siemens Family

William Siemens (above) worked with his brother Frederick to build their improved furnace. They were part of a family that became one of the most important in Germany's road to industrialization. Their older brother Werner founded a company in Berlin to create a telegraph network. The telegraph used electric signals sent along wires. At the time, it was the only form of long-distance communication. Over the decades, Werner Siemens's company grew and made such things as electric streetcars, household appliances, and medical equipment. Today, Siemens is one of the largest companies in the world. Each year, it earns more than $100 billion.

Changing Times

By the time steel was becoming cheaper, industrialization was spreading across Europe and around the world. Northern Italy and Scandinavia were beginning the process. So were parts of eastern Europe and Russia. Great Britain began to lose its lead as the major industrial power in Europe as Germany caught up and then passed it in steel and iron production. As the two leading industrial nations in Europe, Germany and Great Britain began to see themselves as rivals for power. Both countries strengthened their militaries, relying on industry to build new weapons and bigger and more powerful ships.

Factories opened in Scandinavian cities such as Stockholm, Sweden, during the 19th century.

Founded in Italy in 1817, the Lanerossi textile company manufactured wool cloth.

Those two countries and other European nations also competed to acquire colonies, as they had for hundreds of years. In the past, the great kingdoms of Europe sought valuable goods such as gold and rare spices from overseas. During the Industrial Revolution, they sought colonies as a source of natural resources and labor for their industries. The colonies would also buy goods from the countries that controlled them. As the industrialists of Europe sought to make more money, they tied together the economy of the whole world like never before. The Industrial Revolution brought changes no one could have imagined.

MAP OF THE EVENTS

What Happened Where?

Newcastle ←

Manchester, England

...s city was one of the first to industrialize ...ngland, with many textile factories. ...as also the site of a protest against ...king conditions in the factories.

Liverpool **Manchester**

...erpool, England

... Industrial Revolution turned Liverpool ... a major port with many factories. The ... had the world's first elevated railroad ... carried a train powered by electricity.

ENGLAND

Bristol
London

...stol, England

...s city became a major seaport before the ...ustrial Revolution, and its importance ...w during it. Thanks to sea trade and ...ustrialization, its population soared ...ing the 19th century.

Paris

ATLANTIC
OCEAN

London, England

Although not a huge industrial center, London was a major port for sending goods overseas. Events in England's capital influenced the new economy built on factories. Parliament met there and often passed laws that helped industrialization. London banks invested in new companies.

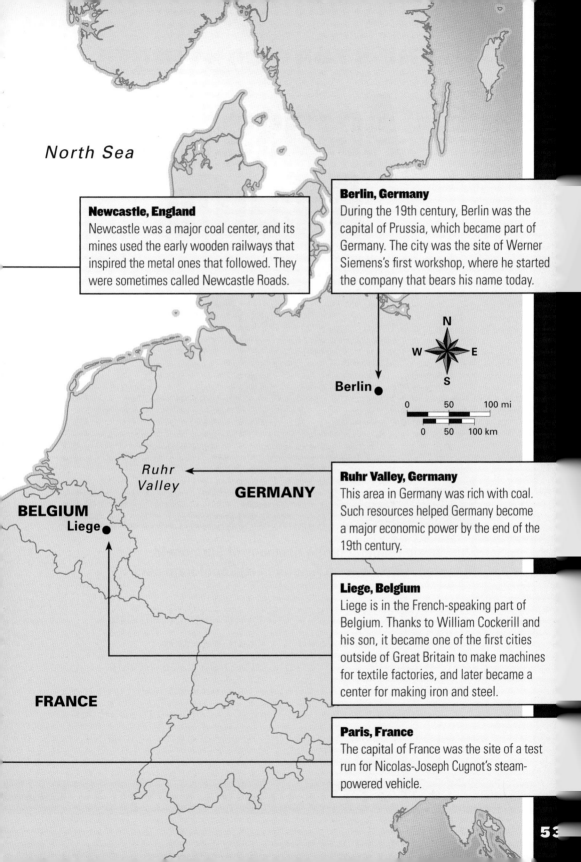

North Sea

Newcastle, England
Newcastle was a major coal center, and its mines used the early wooden railways that inspired the metal ones that followed. They were sometimes called Newcastle Roads.

Berlin, Germany
During the 19th century, Berlin was the capital of Prussia, which became part of Germany. The city was the site of Werner Siemens's first workshop, where he started the company that bears his name today.

Berlin

N
W E
S

0   50   100 mi
0   50   100 km

Ruhr Valley

GERMANY

BELGIUM
Liege

Ruhr Valley, Germany
This area in Germany was rich with coal. Such resources helped Germany become a major economic power by the end of the 19th century.

Liege, Belgium
Liege is in the French-speaking part of Belgium. Thanks to William Cockerill and his son, it became one of the first cities outside of Great Britain to make machines for textile factories, and later became a center for making iron and steel.

FRANCE

Paris, France
The capital of France was the site of a test run for Nicolas-Joseph Cugnot's steam-powered vehicle.

Across the Atlantic

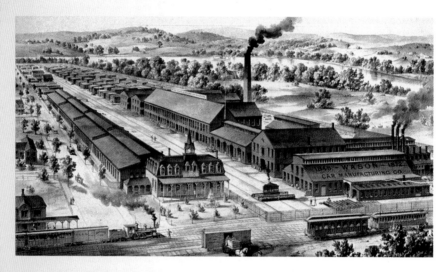

The Wason Manufacturing Company of Springfield, Massachusetts, was an American maker of train cars.

While industrialization went on in Europe, another country across the Atlantic Ocean was also industrializing. Thirteen British colonies in North America had united and won their independence in 1783, creating the United States. The new nation began to spread westward, drawing on the natural resources available. It also attracted Europeans who were seeking jobs. The Industrial Revolution that began in England crossed the ocean and eventually made the United States the greatest industrial power in the world.

Today, some goods once made in America are made in foreign countries where costs are cheaper. However, U.S. factories still produce goods that are sold all over the world. These include airplanes, food products, coal, medical equipment, and electronic products. The United States is also a world leader in creating the software and apps used on millions of computers, smartphones, and tablets. U.S. companies will continue to look for ways to make products faster and cheaper than before, just as the first industrialists did in Europe during the 18th and 19th centuries.

Boeing, an American company, is one of the world's leading airplane manufacturers.

BY WILLIAM E. BOEING IN 1916.

James Watt

Thomas Newcomen (1663–1729) improved on the design of a steam-powered pump made in France. He showed the value of steam engines to industry. His first pump could bring water up from a coal mine 150 feet (46 meters) deep.

Abraham Darby (ca. 1678–1717) ran an ironworks and discovered that smelting iron ore with coke improved the process, as coke could be used in larger furnaces.

Nicolas-Joseph Cugnot (1725–1804) was an engineer for the Austrian army before returning to his homeland of France. There, he invented the first steam-powered vehicle, which had three wheels. A working model of this invention is on display in a Florida auto museum.

Richard Arkwright (1732–1792) was the inventor of a water-powered spinning machine. He built some of the first large textile factories of the Industrial Revolution.

James Watt (1736–1819) was a Scottish inventor who created the steam engine that made it possible to build factories away from water. His engines were used to help make a range of goods, including paper and flour.

Joseph-Marie Jacquard (1752–1834) invented a loom that used punch cards, similar to the ones used to program the first computers. His loom could easily make different patterns in cloth.

William Cockerill (1759–1832) traveled to several European countries before he settled in Belgium, where he became a great industrialist. His company built machines for textile mills.

Richard Trevithick

Richard Trevithick (1771–1833) sought to improve on James Watt's steam engine. He built his own and used it to create the first steam locomotive that ran on tracks.

Henry Bessemer (1813–1898) found a new way to make steel. The Bessemer method of making steel was popular for a time in the United States.

William Siemens (1823–1883) was a German inventor who settled in England because its patent laws helped inventors make money. With his brother Frederick, Siemens invented a new kind of furnace that improved the making of steel.

William Siemens

Pierre-Émile Martin (1824–1915) used the furnace developed by William Siemens to create a new way to make steel. The process was named for both him and Siemens.

TIMELINE

17th Century

English farmers increase crop production; there is an increase in demand for coal as a fuel.

ca. 1705

Thomas Newcomen improves an existing steam engine used to pump water from coal mines.

1709

Abraham Darby uses coke to improve the iron smelting process.

1760s

New machines appear for spinning cotton into thread.

1769

James Watt receives a patent for an improved steam engine; Nicolas-Joseph Cugnot designs a steam-powered car.

1780s

Richard Arkwright uses steam engines to power machines in his textile factories.

1804

Joseph-Marie Jacquard designs a loom that is controlled by punch cards.

1815

The end of major wars in Europe helps spread industrialization on the European continent.

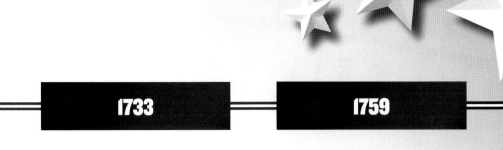

1733

The flying shuttle helps speed up production of cloth on looms.

1759

Parliament passes a law to build a new canal near Manchester.

1795

Workers burn down a mill in Manchester to protest the new technology that reduced the number of textile jobs.

1802

Parliament passes a law designed to protect orphans sent to work in factories.

1803

Richard Trevithick uses a small steam-powered locomotive on a railway at a coal mine.

1825

George Stephenson builds the first railroad to carry passengers between two cities.

1856

Henry Bessemer discovers a new way to make steel faster than before.

1864

Pierre-Émile Martin uses a furnace designed by William Siemens to create another new method for making steel.

LIVING HISTORY

Primary sources provide firsthand evidence about a topic. Witnesses to a historical event create primary sources. They include autobiographies, newspaper reports of the time, oral histories, photographs, and memoirs. A secondary source analyzes primary sources and is one step or more removed from the event. Secondary sources include textbooks, encyclopedias, and commentaries. To view the following primary and secondary sources, go to www.factsfornow.scholastic.com. Enter the keywords **European Industrial Revolution** and look for the Living History logo Σι.

Σι **Coalbrookdale by Night** During the Industrial Revolution, many artists documented the changing landscape of Europe. Philip James de Loutherbourg's painting *Coalbrookdale by Night* shows the smoke and flames that came along with industrialization.

Σι **The *Mechanics' Magazine*** The *Mechanics' Magazine* was a publication devoted to documenting new inventions and innovations in the 19th century. Back issues of the magazine, widely available online, provide an important record of the progress made during the Industrial Revolution.

Σι **Stephenson's *Rocket*** The *Rocket* locomotive, built by George Stephenson and his son, Robert, was one of the fastest locomotives of its time. *Rocket* is now on display at the Science Museum in London, England.

Σι **Tull's Seed Drill** Jethro Tull's seed drill allowed farmers to more quickly and easily plant neat rows of seeds. It was among the many innovations that would eventually lead to the Industrial Revolution. A model of Tull's seed drill is on display at the Science Museum in London, England.

RESOURCES

Books

Allport, Alan. *The British Industrial Revolution*. New York: Chelsea House, 2011.

Burgan, Michael. *American Capitalism*. New York: Children's Press, 2013.

Hicks, Peter. *Documenting the Industrial Revolution*. New York: Rosen Central, 2010.

Mattern, Joanne. *The Birth of the Locomotive (1780–1820)*. Hockessin, DE: Mitchell Lane Publishers, 2013.

McDaniel, Melissa. *The Industrial Revolution*. New York: Children's Press, 2012.

Orr, Tamra. *The Steam Engine*. New York: Franklin Watts, 2005.

Samuels, Charlie. *Timeline of the Industrial Revolution*. New York: Gareth Stevens Publishing, 2010.

Whiting, Jim. *James Watt and the Steam Engine*. Hockessin, DE: Mitchell Lane Publishers, 2006.

Visit this Scholastic Web site for more information on the European industrial revolution:
www.factsfornow.scholastic.com
Enter the keywords European Industrial Revolution

GLOSSARY

agricultural (ag-ri-KUL-chur-uhl) having to do with farming

canals (kuh-NALZ) channels that are dug across land so that boats can travel between two bodies of water

economy (i-KAHN-uh-mee) the system of buying, selling, making things, and managing money in a place

engineers (en-juh-NEERZ) people who are specially trained to design and build machines or large structures such as bridges and roads

fossil fuel (FAH-suhl FYOOL) coal, oil, or natural gas formed from the remains of prehistoric plants and animals

industrial (in-DUH-stree-uhl) having to do with factories and making things in large quantities

investing (in-VEST-ing) giving or lending money to something, such as a company, with the intention of getting more money back later

labor (LAY-bur) work, especially physical work

molten (MOHL-tuhn) melted at a high temperature; usually describing metal or rock

patent (PA-tent) a legal document giving the inventor of an item the sole right to manufacture or sell it

smelting (SMELT-ing) the process of using heat to remove metal from the rocks in which it is found

textiles (TEK-stilez) woven or knitted fabrics or cloths

unions (YOON-yuhnz) organized groups of workers set up to help improve working conditions, wages, and health benefits

INDEX

Page numbers in *italics* indicate illustrations.

ABOUT THE AUTHOR

Michael Burgan is the author of more than 250 books for children and young adults, both fiction and nonfiction. His works include biographies of U.S. and world leaders and histories of the American Revolution, World War II, and the Cold War. A graduate of the University of Connecticut with a degree in history, Burgan is also a produced playwright and the editor of the *Biographer's Craft*, the newsletter of Biographers International Organization (BIO). He lives in Santa Fe, New Mexico.